D1517302

Heinemann InfoSearch

Uranus, Neptune, and Pluto

Tim Goss

Heinemann Library
Chicago, Illinois

Layout by Roslyn Broder
Illustrations by Calvin J. Hamilton
Printed in Hong Kong

07 06 05 04 03
10 9 8 7 6 5 4 3 2 1

Library of Congress Cataloging-in-Publication Data
Goss, Tim, 1958-
  Uranus, Neptune, and Pluto / Tim Goss.
      p. cm. -- (The universe)
Summary: Presents information about the three outer planets of Uranus,
Neptune, and Pluto, including when and how they were discovered, what is
currently known about them, and relevant spacecraft expeditions.
Includes bibliographical references and index.
  ISBN 1-58810-918-6 (HC)   1-4034-0619-7 (Pbk)
  1. Uranus (Planet)--Juvenile literature. 2. Neptune
(Planet)--Juvenile literature. 3. Pluto (Planet)--Juvenile literature.
[1. Uranus (Planet) 2. Neptune (Planet) 3. Pluto (Planet) 4. Planets.]
I. Title. II. Series.
  QB681 .G69 2002
  523.47--dc21
                              2002001520

Acknowledgments
The author and publisher are grateful to the following for permission to reproduce copyright
material: p. 4 NASA/Ames Research Center/Rick Guidice; pp. 5, 23 Alan Stern/Southwest Research
Institute, Marc Buie/Lowell Observatory, NASA and ESA; p. 6 D. Van Ravenswaay/Photo Researchers,
Inc.; pp. 7, 10 Bettman/Corbis; p. 8 Hulton-Deutsch Collection/Corbis; p. 9 Mary Evans Picture
Library; pp. 11, 24, 25 Courtesy of Calvin J. Hamilton/www.solarviews.com; pp. 12, 13, 15R, 16, 18,
20, 21, 26, 28, 29 NASA/JPL/Caltech; p. 14 Dr. R. Albrecht, ESA/ESO Space Telescope European
Coordinating Facility, and NASA; p. 15L Kenneth Seidelmann/U.S. Naval Observatory and NASA; p.
17 Nordic Optical Telescope Scientific Association; p. 19 Erich Karkoschka/University of Arizona
Lunar & Planetary Lab and NASA; p. 22 H. Hammel/Massachusetts Institute of Technology and
NASA; p. 27 Eliot Young/Southwest Research Institute et al., and NASA

Cover photograph by NASA/JPL/Caltech

The publisher would like to thank Geza Gyuk and Diana Challis of the Adler Planetarium for their
comments in the preparation of this book.

Every effort has been made to contact copyright holders of any material reproduced in this book.
Any omissions will be rectified in subsequent printings if notice is given to the publisher.

Some words are shown in bold, **like this.** You can find out what
they mean by looking in the glossary.

Contents

Where in the Sky Are Uranus, Neptune, and Pluto?

Uranus, Neptune, and Pluto are **planets** seven, eight, and nine in our **solar system.** These three planets are often called the Outer Planets. Jupiter and Saturn are sometimes grouped with the Outer Planets as well.

On a clear night, you might be able to see Uranus with **binoculars.** It is almost 1,700 million miles (2,700 million kilometers) from Earth. Neptune is about 2,700 million miles (4,300 million kilometers) from Earth. You can only see it with a **telescope.** Pluto is at times more than two and a half billion miles (4 billion kilometers) from Earth. You cannot see it very well from Earth, even with a telescope.

The Outer Planets are the ones farthest from the Sun.

The solar system
The solar system is made of all the planets, **moons, comets,** and **asteroids** that circle the **Sun.** The Sun's **gravity** pulls on all of the objects in our solar system. If it were not for the pull of the Sun, the planets would travel in straight lines. This would send them out into deep space! The force of gravity keeps the planets in regular paths around the Sun called **orbits.**

What is the Hubble Space Telescope?

The Hubble Space Telescope is above Earth's atmosphere. This is important because the atmosphere can distort, or change, our view of the stars and planets from Earth. An antenna on the telescope sends the information it gathers to a **satellite.** The satellite then sends the information to scientists on Earth.

Why is it so hard to find the Outer Planets?

Uranus, Neptune, and Pluto are so far away from the Sun that very little sunlight reaches them. The small amount of sunlight the planets **reflect** is not enough for them to be easily visible from Earth.

Think of what it is like to sit by a campfire. The people closest to the fire get the most warmth from it. In the same way, the planets closest to the Sun get more light and heat from it than the ones that are farther away. It is easiest for people on Earth to see the planets that are reflecting the most sunlight.

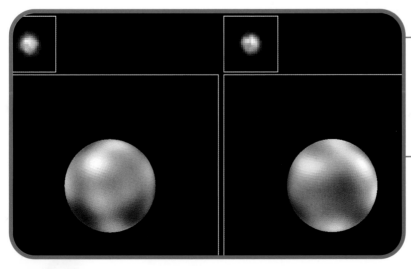

The best views of Pluto have come from the Hubble Space Telescope.

Years and years and years

Earth's **orbit** around the **Sun** takes about 365 **days.** We call that time period one Earth **year.** Uranus needs about 84 Earth years to complete one orbit. Neptune needs 164 Earth years to complete one orbit. It takes Pluto about 248 Earth years to orbit the Sun.

The Outer Planets have farther to go in their orbits around the Sun. They have to make a larger circle because they are so far away.

Not like a day on Earth

One day is the time is takes for a **planet** to spin around one time on its **axis.** On Earth, one day is 24 hours long. The length of a day on Uranus or Neptune is much shorter. A Uranus day is about seventeen hours long, and Neptune's day is about sixteen hours.

Pluto spins very slowly and its day is much longer than an Earth day. One day on Pluto is as long as about six and one third Earth days. That is almost one week on Earth.

How was Uranus discovered?

An **astronomer** named William Herschel found Uranus in 1781. He had been searching the night skies with his **telescope** to study **stars.** At first, Herschel thought Uranus was a **comet** or star. Earlier astronomers who had seen it thought it was another star. In 1690, one astronomer even named this "new star." However, Herschel observed that it did not have a tail like a comet. It also moved slowly, showing that it must be in an orbit. This meant that it had to be a planet, not a star.

William Herschel was born in Germany but was living in England when he discovered the planet Uranus. His sister Caroline took notes on his findings.

How were the planets named?

Uranus was named after the Greek god of the heavens. The god Uranus was the father of Saturn and the grandfather of Jupiter. Neptune is named for the Roman god of the sea. Pluto is the Roman god of the underworld.

How was Neptune discovered?

No one had ever seen Neptune before it was discovered in 1846. One reason is that it cannot be seen without a **telescope.** The other reason is that until Uranus was discovered, **astronomers** thought that the first six **planets** were the whole **solar system.** So, no one had even looked for more planets.

John Couch Adams (1819–1892) was one of the people who discovered the planet Neptune.

William Herschel and others had noticed that the **orbit** of Uranus was different than what they expected. Uranus moved as if forces other than those from the **Sun** and the other planets were affecting its orbit. This suggested that another planet might be there.

Two mathematicians, John Couch Adams in England in 1843 and Urbain-Jean-Joseph Le Verrier in France in 1846, began to use mathematical formulas to figure out the position of another planet that could be affecting Uranus's orbit. Both mathematicians sent their predictions of where there might be another planet to astronomers.

The astronomer in England to whom Adams sent his findings did not have charts showing the **stars** in that part of the sky. He had to make his own chart and then check the sky each night to see if one of the "stars" had moved. If it did, he would know that it was a planet, not a star.

A German astronomer named Johann Gottfried Galle received Le Verrier's information on September 23, 1846. Galle already had maps of the stars. That night he and his assistant looked at the part of the sky where Le Verrier thought there might be another planet and found a new "star." The next night they saw that the star had moved. Galle knew they had discovered the eighth planet.

This engraving shows Le Verrier explaining the discovery of Neptune to French King Louis Philippe.

How was Pluto discovered?

Astronomers had thought there might be a **planet** beyond Uranus because of the path of Uranus's **orbit.** Soon the pattern of Neptune's movements led scientists to think there was another planet beyond it. Scientists discovered the ninth planet 84 years after finding Neptune. One reason it took so long was that better **telescopes** had to be invented to find an object hundreds of millions of miles away. Pluto is also very small compared to the other planets. That makes it more difficult to find with a telescope.

In the early 1900s, an American astronomer, Percival Lowell, led the search from an **observatory** in Arizona. A young **amateur** astronomer named Clyde Tombaugh continued the search when Lowell died in 1916. He used a new telescope built in 1929 just for this project. He took photographs of the sky and compared them from night to night. On February 18, 1930, Tombaugh found something in the photos that looked like a very dim **star.** However, it was moving very slowly, and stars do not move. Tombaugh had discovered the planet Pluto.

The moving "star" that Clyde Tombaugh located was actually the planet we now know as Pluto.

Are the Outer Planets All the Same?

Pluto's orbit path is very different

The orbits of Uranus and Neptune are almost perfect circles. Pluto's orbit has an oval shape. That means it looks like a long, stretched-out circle. At one point in its orbit, Pluto crosses Neptune's orbit. At that point, Pluto is closer to the **Sun** than Neptune is.

Uranus and Pluto are tipped over

Each planet is tilted on its **axis.** That means that the planet leans to one side. Most planets just lean a little. The tilt of Earth as it moves around the Sun causes the seasons. Neptune's tilt is almost the same as Earth's. Uranus leans so much that the planet is on its side. Instead of the north pole being at the top of the planet and the south pole being at the bottom, Uranus's **equator** runs from top to bottom. Pluto tilts even more than Uranus.

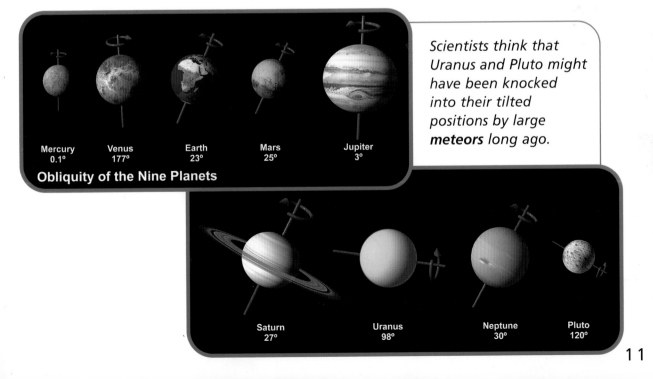

| Mercury | Venus | Earth | Mars | Jupiter |
| 0.1º | 177º | 23º | 25º | 3º |

Obliquity of the Nine Planets

| Saturn | Uranus | Neptune | Pluto |
| 27º | 98º | 30º | 120º |

Scientists think that Uranus and Pluto might have been knocked into their tilted positions by large meteors long ago.

Three planets, two colors

Uranus and Neptune are two of the four **planets** known as the **Gas** Giants. The other two are Jupiter and Saturn. The way the **methane** gas in their **atmospheres** is affected by light makes Uranus and Neptune look blue. Light from the **Sun** is made of waves of different colors. You can see these colors when there is a rainbow in the sky. When the Sun shines on Uranus and Neptune, the methane soaks up the red parts of the light. The light that is left is **reflected** back into space. We see that light as blue light.

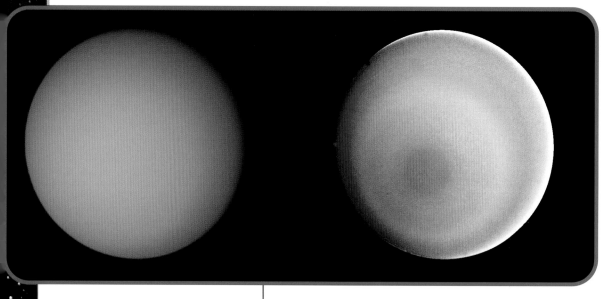

Uranus is shown in true color on the left. Color filters were used in the image on the right to show the different zones in the atmosphere.

Pluto is not a gas planet. It has a solid surface covered with ice. Some photos show that Pluto is reddish brown. Parts of Pluto look whitish, perhaps from frost.

The Outer Planets are big and small

Uranus is the third largest planet in our **solar system.** Only Saturn and Jupiter are larger. If Uranus was empty, about 61 Earths could fit inside it. Neptune is also much bigger than Earth. About 58 Earths could fit inside of Neptune. Pluto is the smallest planet in our solar system. Pluto is so small that you could put over 150 Plutos inside of an empty Earth.

Uranus and Neptune have lots of moons

Uranus has at least 21 **moons.** William Herschel discovered the first two, Titania and Oberon, in 1787. Ten moons were found by the *Voyager 2* **space probe** in 1985 and 1986. The last three were not found until 1999. There could be more. Uranus's moon Miranda is very strange. It has more **craters,** canyons, and high cliffs than other moons. Scientists think it may have been an object that was broken apart at one time. Then the pieces came back together to form a new moon.

Oberon—Uranus's outermost moon—has an icy surface covered with craters.

Neptune has at least eight **moons.** Six moons were discovered by *Voyager 2* in 1989. The largest moon is Triton. It was found in 1846, about two weeks after the **planet** was discovered. Most moons **orbit** their planets in the same direction as the planet is turning on its **axis.** Triton orbits Neptune in the opposite direction. It is one of just two moons in our solar system that do this. Phoebe, one of Saturn's moons, is the other. Triton is also the coldest place in the **solar system** ever visited by a spacecraft. The temperature on Triton's surface is about –391°F (–235°C). It is likely that Pluto is even colder than that during most of its orbit around the Sun.

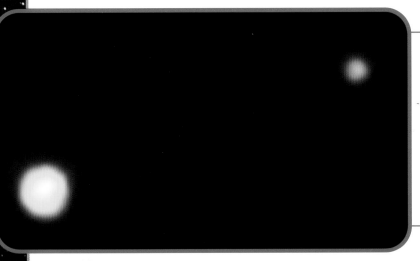

*Pluto and its moon are so close that photographs taken from Earth show only one object. Only photographs taken from the Hubble Space **Telescope** clearly show the planet and its moon as separate objects.*

Pluto has one moon

Pluto's only moon is called Charon. Its orbit is very close to Pluto and the moon tilts on its side just like Pluto. The time it takes Charon to orbit Pluto is equal to the time it takes for Pluto to rotate once on its axis. If you were standing on Pluto, you would always see the same side of Charon.

Uranus and Neptune have rings

Almost 200 years after Uranus was discovered, scientists learned that it has rings. In 1977, scientists in the National Aeronautics and Space Administration's (NASA's) Kuiper Airborne **Observatory** discovered six rings. **Astronomers** in an observatory in Australia found three different rings on the same day. In 1986, *Voyager 2* found two more rings.

Neptune also has a ring system made of dust particles. There may be as many six main rings and some smaller ones. They are hard to see from Earth. *Voyager 2's* pictures gave scientists more information about the rings.

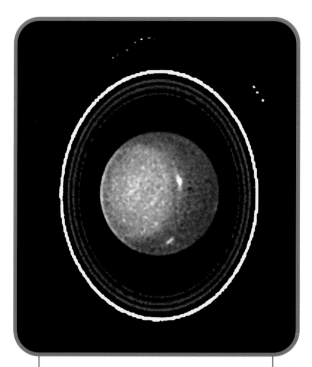

Uranus's rings are much darker than those of Jupiter or Saturn.

This photo shows Neptune's ring system.

How's the Weather on Uranus, Neptune, and Pluto?

Uranus and Neptune

Uranus's seasons are more than twenty Earth **years** long. This is because the **planet** is tilted on its side during its 84-year **orbit** around the **Sun.** As Uranus **revolves,** the Sun shines on one pole for about twenty years. During this time, the other half of the planet is in darkness. Then it shines on the **equator** for the same period of time. Next, it shines on the other pole and, finally, the other side of the equator.

Since the orbit is almost a perfect circle, and Uranus is so far from the Sun, there is not much difference in temperature between the sunny and dark parts. Near the top of the clouds, the average temperature is about –346°F (–210°C).

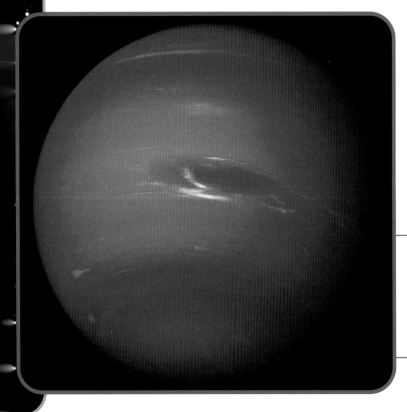

On Neptune, not even the parts that are tilted toward the Sun get warm.

Neptune's **axis** is tilted almost like Earth's. However, it is so far from the Sun that it does not have seasons. The round orbit means that the planet is almost always the same distance from the Sun. Neptune's temperature at the top of the clouds is about −364°F (−220°C).

Pluto

Even though no **space probe** has ever visited Pluto, **satellites** and the Hubble Space **Telescope** have given us some information. The usual surface temperature seems to be about −382°F (−230°C). Sometimes it gets even colder than that. On Uranus and Neptune, the temperature does not change much from "season to season" because

This is an example of the best image of Pluto that can be taken from Earth.

they are so far from the Sun. If Pluto is even farther away, why does it have changes in temperature? The answer is in the orbit. Pluto's orbit is a very long stretched-out circle called an oval. When it is at the far end of the orbit, very far away from the Sun, it gets much colder.

Is there air on the Outer Planets?

We think of air as being **gases** that we can breathe. On Earth, the air we breathe is a mixture of **nitrogen** and **oxygen.** Of the two gases, oxygen is the one we need to breathe.

The Outer **Planets** also have a mix of gases in their **atmospheres.** However, you cannot breathe the air on Uranus, Neptune, or Pluto, because there is no oxygen.

The atmospheres of Uranus and Neptune

The atmospheres of Uranus and Neptune are made up mostly of **hydrogen** and **helium** gas. Uranus and Neptune also have a small amount of water and **methane** gas in their upper atmospheres. Uranus has a tiny bit of **ammonia** in its atmosphere. Uranus's clouds are the brightest of all the Outer Planets.

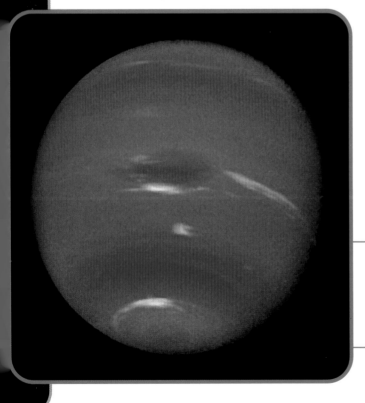

Neptune's blue-green atmosphere has clouds scattered throughout.

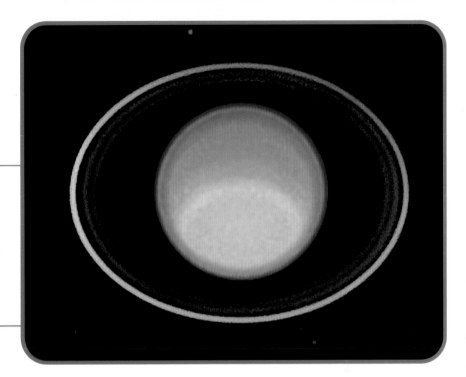

Color filters were used in this image to show the layers of Uranus's atmosphere.

Scientists think that the atmospheres of Uranus and Neptune have three main layers of clouds below the outer methane cloud layer. The top layer is made of ammonia clouds. The middle cloud layer is made from ammonia and **sulfur.** The bottom cloud layer of each planet is probably made of frozen water.

Pluto's atmosphere

Pluto's thin atmosphere is mostly made of nitrogen gas with much smaller amounts of methane gas and **carbon monoxide** gas. Scientists did not know for sure that Pluto had an atmosphere until 1988. **Astronomers** on Earth watched Pluto move in front of a **star.** Before the star disappeared behind the planet, it looked less bright. The gases in Pluto's atmosphere covered the star before the planet did. It was like looking at a bright light through a smoky haze.

Odd things about Pluto's atmosphere

Pluto's **atmosphere** extends very high up because Pluto's **gravity** is not strong enough to hold it close to the **planet.** If you weighed 90 pounds (41 kilograms) on Earth, you would weigh only six pounds (about three kilograms) on Pluto. Pluto is so cold that its atmosphere may only be in a **gas** state when the planet is closest to the **Sun.** When Pluto is farther from the Sun, the gases probably freeze into ice, leaving Pluto without an atmosphere.

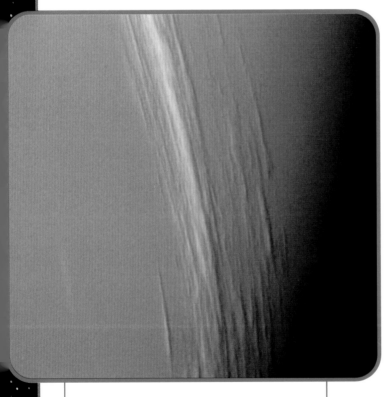

Cloud streaks in Neptune's atmosphere range from 31 to 124 miles (50 to 200 kilometers) across.

Windy weather

Based on the information scientists have so far, Uranus seems to have fewer storms than any of the Gas Giant planets. The storms it does have, though, involve high wind speeds. In 1999, pictures from the Hubble Space **Telescope** showed storm patterns on Uranus moving the clouds at more than 300 miles (500 kilometers) per hour.

Neptune has the fastest winds of any planet. In 1989, *Voyager 2* found a storm system that scientists named the Great Dark Spot. It was as big as Earth and moved at about 745 miles (1,200 kilometers) per hour. The Great Dark Spot later disappeared, but another large spot was found in 1997. *Voyager 2* also found a small, fast-moving cloud that blows around the planet every sixteen hours. Scientists studying it have named it the Scooter.

Neptune's most recognizable features are the Great Dark Spot, the Scooter (just below the Great Dark Spot), and what is known as Dark Spot 2 (farther down).

One reason for Neptune's fast winds may be that it gives off more heat than it gets from the Sun. This heat warms the air as it escapes. The warm air rises and pushes around the colder air, creating winds.

We will have to wait for a **space probe** to visit Pluto to learn more about its winds. So far, scientists think that conditions are calm on Pluto.

What Would I See if I Went to the Outer Planets?

An ocean as far as the eye can see

Uranus and Neptune are **Gas** Giants and do not have solid surfaces. The **atmosphere** of Uranus gets thicker and thicker until it becomes a part liquid, part "icy" material. The liquid is made of water, **methane,** and **ammonia.** If you had a spaceship that could explore oceans as well as outer space, you would see that the liquid material extends deep into the **planet.** Neptune has an ocean similar to the one on Uranus.

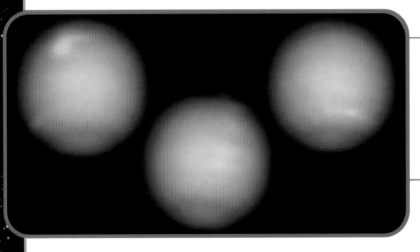

These three images of Neptune show the movement of the planet's clouds.

Bring your ice skates to Pluto

Pluto's surface is covered with ice made of frozen methane, frozen **carbon monoxide,** and some **nitrogen.** Some of the gases in the atmosphere freeze when the planet is at its farthest point from the **Sun.** When Pluto is closer to the Sun, those parts of the atmosphere become gas again. The methane ice **reflects** a lot of light and makes Pluto look bright. The Hubble Space **Telescope** has shown that Pluto has **polar caps** at the top and bottom parts of the planet.

How can ice be hot?

For a scientist, "icy" does not always refer to what we think of as ice. The term can also be used to describe the composition of a material, or the general qualities of something. The "icy" parts of the ocean on Uranus and Neptune are not frozen water. They are simply more solid pieces of material floating in the hot liquid. They are similar in appearance to ice floating in water, but they are actually very hot.

Polar caps are huge pieces of ice that form on the top and bottom parts of a planet where it does not get much sunlight. The Hubble Space Telescope also found dark spots near Pluto's **equator.** Scientists are not sure yet what the spots are.

A map like this can help scientists study the high and low points on the surface of Pluto.

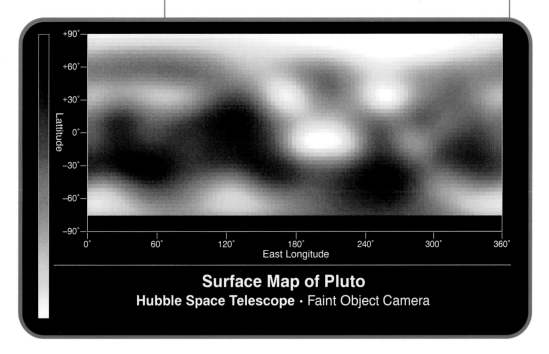

Surface Map of Pluto
Hubble Space Telescope · Faint Object Camera

What's Inside Uranus, Neptune, and Pluto?

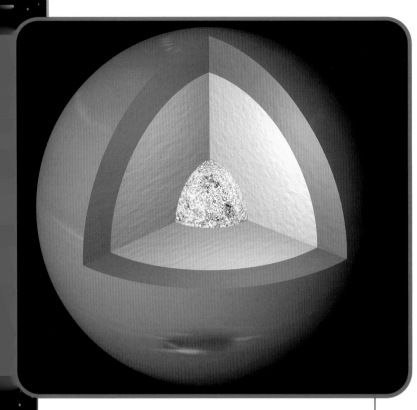

Neptune does not actually have clearly defined layers like this diagram. They blend into one another. This diagram helps give us a general idea of where changes take place.

Some **planets,** such as Earth and Mars, have clear lines between their **atmosphere, crust, mantle,** and **core.** With the **Gas** Giants, there is not a clear line between the atmosphere and the rest of the planet. It is more of a gradual change. Pluto, the only Outer Planet that is not a Gas Giant, does have separate layers inside.

Uranus and Neptune are liquid on the inside

In the thicker, deeper part of the atmosphere of Uranus and Neptune, each planet is made of materials that are part "ice" and part liquid. This is what we call the ocean on these planets. Beneath the ocean-like atmosphere, the cores of the planets are rocky.

How is Uranus different from the other Gas Giants?

When the planets first formed long ago, all of their inside parts were very hot. Over time, each planet slowly cooled down. The heat in their cores flowed to the outside of the planet. That is still happening to three of the Gas Giant planets. But Uranus is different from the other planets because its core does not give off very much heat. Scientists do not yet know why Uranus is different in this way.

What is inside Pluto?

Scientists know very little about Pluto because it is so far away from Earth. Under Pluto's icy surface and crust, there may be a mantle of water ice. Under that, the planet may have a rocky core. Scientists believe that Pluto's rocky core makes up over half of the planet.

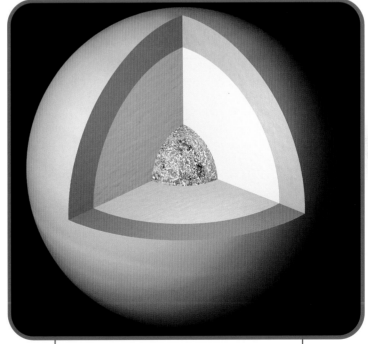

Uranus does not have clearly defined layers, either. The atmosphere changes gradually, as it does on Neptune.

Could I Ever Go to the Outer Planets?

Are you sure you want to go?

Voyager 2 took almost eight and a half years to get to Uranus. That includes the time it spent visiting Jupiter and Saturn along the way. After leaving Uranus, *Voyager 2* needed three and a half more years to get to Neptune. No **space probe** has been to Pluto.

Voyager 2 *took one of the first images of Neptune's rings.*

Suppose that there was a spacecraft that could support people on the long voyage to the Outer Planets. There would still be problems to worry about.

Imagine that you needed to talk to the people at the space center on Earth right away. It would take more than five hours for your message to reach them if you were close to Neptune. Then it would take just as long for their answer to get back to you.

Visiting Uranus and Neptune with *Voyager 2*

Even though visits by people to the Outer Planets are not possible at this time, we have still been able to learn a lot about Uranus and Neptune. The *Voyager 2* space probe found ten new **moons** and two more rings around Uranus. It also found six more moons and three more rings around Neptune.

Pluto will finally get a visitor

NASA is planning a space mission to Pluto. They will send a space probe to Pluto and its moon, Charon. It will take at least eight years to get there. Scientists hope to learn about Pluto and Charon's **atmospheres,** surfaces, and interiors during this **flyby** mission. Beyond Pluto, there may be more objects to visit. No one knows how far space travel will take us.

This image shows Pluto's true color. The image looks blurry because it is made up of many smaller images put together. Scientists have a hard time getting clear images of Pluto because it is so far away from Earth.

Fact File

Average distance from the Sun
Earth	93 million miles (150 million kilometers)
Uranus	1.8 billion miles (2.9 billion kilometers)
Neptune	2.8 billion miles (4.5 billion kilometers)
Pluto	3.7 billion miles (6.0 billion kilometers)

Length of a year
Earth	1 Earth year
Uranus	84 Earth years
Neptune	164 Earth years
Pluto	248 Earth years

Diameter at the equator
Earth	7,926 miles (12,756 kilometers)
Uranus	31,770 miles (51,118 kilometers)
Neptune	30,809 miles (49,572 kilometers)
Pluto	1,430 miles (2,300 kilometers)

Length of one day
Earth	24 hours
Uranus	17 hours
Neptune	16 hours
Pluto	6 1/3 Earth days

Triton is one of Neptune's moons. In this image, color filters show the details on the moon's surface.

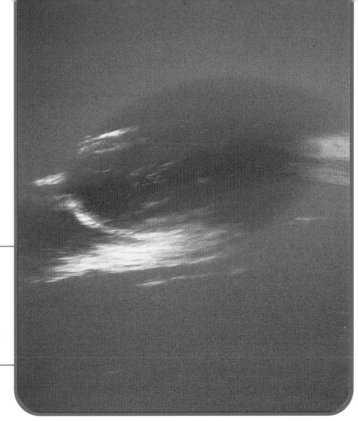

Neptune's spiral-shaped Great Dark Spot is probably a storm that rotates counterclockwise.

Atmosphere

Earth	nitrogen, oxygen
Uranus	hydrogen, helium, and methane gas
Neptune	hydrogen, helium, and methane gas
Pluto	nitrogen and methane

Number of moons and rings

Earth	1 moon and no rings
Uranus	21 moons and 11 rings
Neptune	8 moons and 5 rings
Pluto	1 moon and no rings

Temperature range

Earth's surface	–92°F (–69°C) to 136°F (58°C)
Uranus	–346°F (–210°C) to ??? (increases with depth)
Neptune	–364°F (–220°C) to ??? (increases with depth)
Pluto	about –382°F (about –230°C)

Glossary

amateur   someone who does something as a hobby that other people do as a career

ammonia   strong-smelling gas found in the atmospheres of many planets; a substance used on Earth to make chemicals and cleaning products

asteroid   large piece of floating rock that formed at the same time as the planets and orbits the Sun

astronomer   person who studies objects in outer space

atmosphere   all of the gases that surround an object in outer space

axis   imaginary line through the middle of an object in space, around which it spins as it rotates

binoculars   handheld equipment used for seeing things more closely

carbon monoxide   gas made up of a mixture of carbon and oxygen

comet   ball of ice and rock that orbits around the Sun

core   material at the center of a planet

crater   bowl-shaped hole in the ground that is made by a meteorite or a burst of lava

crust   top, solid layer of an object in outer space. The outer part of the crust is called the surface.

day   time it takes for a planet to spin on its axis one time

equator   imaginary line around the middle of a planet

flyby   mission to a planet in which the spaceship does not land

gas   substance that makes up a planet's atmosphere

gravity   invisible force that pulls an object toward the center of another object in space

helium   gas found on many planets; used on Earth to make balloons float in the air

hydrogen   substance found on many planets. On Earth, hydrogen gas mixes with oxygen gas to form water.

mantle   middle layer of a planet or moon. It lies between the core and the crust.

meteor   piece of rock or dust that travels in outer space

methane   gas found in the atmosphere of some planets in our solar system

moon   object that floats in an orbit around a planet

nitrogen   gas found in the atmosphere of Earth and some of the other planets in our solar system

observatory   place with high-powered telescopes where astronomers study the stars and planets

orbit   curved path of one object in space moving around another object; or, to take such a path under the influence of gravity

oxygen   gas that is found in the atmospheres of many planets; gas that humans and animals breathe in

planet large object in space that orbits a central star, has an atmosphere, and does not produce its own light

polar cap large piece of ice that covers the north or south pole of a planet and does not receive much sunlight

reflect bounce back

revolve travel one time around the Sun; or for a moon to travel one time around a planet

satellite shortened version of the term artificial satellite, meaning a machine made to orbit Earth

solar system group of objects in space that all float in orbits around a central star

space probe ship that carries computers and other instruments to study objects in outer space

star burning ball of gases in outer space that produces light and energy through a process of chemical change

sulfur yellow-colored, powdery material; found on many planets in gas form

Sun central star in our solar system

telescope instrument used by astronomers to study objects in outer space

year time it takes for a planet to complete one orbit around the Sun

More Books to Read

Brimner, Larry Dane. *Neptune.* Danbury, Conn.: Children's Press, 1999.

Brimner, Larry Dane. *Pluto.* Danbury, Conn.: Children's Press, 1999.

Brimner, Larry Dane. *Uranus.* Danbury, Conn.: Children's Press, 1999.

Kerrod, Robin. *Uranus, Neptune, and Pluto.* Minneapolis, Minn.: Lerner Publishing Group, 2000.

Index